ACKNOWLEDGEMENTS

I would like to acknowledge anyone who has ever been courageous enough to fail, fail fast, and fail forward on their course to success.

DEDICATIONS

This book is dedicated first and foremost to the people in my life who gave me a hand when I needed to be lifted up from my own moments of failure. To my parents who always challenged me to put myself out there and didn't make me stop when I failed but rather encouraged me to get back up and try again. To new failures that will catapult me towards this next phase of my greatest life successes.

FAILURE IS NOT THE OPPOSITE OF SUCCESS, IT'S PART OF SUCCESS!

PATRICK WILLIAMS

RAVE REVIEWS

"Patrick has unlocked the single most critical barrier to personal and financial success. Fear is what stops people from living the life of their dreams. By making it ok to fail, and indeed illustrating how successful people fail regularly, people will become more confident when they know it's ok to fail; and since confidence breeds success, this book should become the successful person's bible." — Ron Miller, Chairman of the Board, StartEngine; Forbes: "Crowdfunding Just Got More Exciting", LA Times: "Equity Crowdfunding Lets Start-ups Sell Shares To Average Joe"

"I have always embraced my failures because I was set up with them from the start. It has made me who I am. This book is a good reminder and an inspiration to never forget this!" — Lisa D., Shark Tank Entrepreneur, Winner of America's Top Model

"After reading just the first few chapters of Patrick's book, I can't wait to finish it. As a consultant in the IT world, I'm always thinking about failure. Thanks to Patrick, I now look at failure as part of the Journey." — Tyler Lay, Business Owner

"Talk about INSPIRATION! Who knew failure was actually a main ingredient to success? We're lead to believe we're suppose to avoid failure. Not so! Patrick says to go for it and success will come no matter. Don't be afraid. Failure is just a mile marker on the road to where you're going." — Bart Smith, Author/Speaker

"This is a must read for anyone who aims to be at the top of their field. Patrick proves that failures are not negative, but stepping stones to success." — Dan Smith, Author, Public Speaker, Strategist

"Failure is the key to success. We learn from each mistake and ultimately fail into success. Patrick Williams equips readers with a simply admonishment; I HOPE YOU FAIL, and success will be your by-product." — Rev. Marcus Murchinson, Founder, Watts Up

COPYRIGHT NOTICE

Failing To Success is protected by copyright law. The contents of this book may not be reproduced or transmitted in any form or by any means, electronic or mechanical, including photocopying, recording or by any information storage and retrieval system without written permission from the authors, except for the inclusion of brief quotations in a review.

© 2020 by Patrick Williams

ALL RIGHTS RESERVED WORLDWIDE

ISBN-13: 979-8623987181

For more information about *Failing To Success,* individual orders; bundled orders, discounts for bulk-quantity purchases; audio products; interviews; information on seminars; JV opportunities; mentoring/consulting; booking Patrick Williams to speak at your next seminar, workshop or event; please contact the author at his website:

www.Failing2Success.com

TABLE OF CONTENTS

FOREWARD

MESSAGE FROM THE AUTHOR

PART 1 – WHAT IS FAILING TO SUCCESS?

PART 2 – WHY FAIL TO SUCCESS?

PART 3 – BELIEVE IN YOURSELF

PART 4 – TAKE ACTION!

PART 5 – ENTREPRENEURS

PART 6 – YOU ARE YOUR ART

PART 7 – THE FALL & RISE OF AMAZON & JEFF BEZOS

PART 8 – AN AMAZING RACE & FACING ADVERSITY ON TV

PART 9 – THE MOST FAILING PLAYER IN BASKETBALL

PART 10 – THE CLICHÉ OF THE STRUGGLING ARTIST

PART 11 – MEASURING SUCCESS – WHERE DOES IT START?

PART 12 – REMARKABLE STORY OF THOMAS A. EDISON

PART 13 – THE SHORTCUT TO SUCCESS

PART 14 – HURRY UP & FAIL!

SUMMARY & WRAP-UP

ABOUT THE AUTHOR

PATRICK WILLIAMS is a seasoned entrepreneur who has started and built many businesses throughout his career.

With this vast and varied experience, Patrick brings calmness and clarity to any business situation.

PATRICK WILLIAMS

Patrick's primary focus has been building companies from various real estate businesses, even national service companies to restaurants. His customer-focused mindset helped him build a multi-million dollar business.

Patrick's ability to provide workable solutions to challenging situations makes him an invaluable asset to teams looking to expand their business and grow their revenue.

As a student of failing to success, Patrick took his experience and knowledge to author this book where he shares how failure is an inevitable and necessary part on the path to success.

MESSAGE FROM THE AUTHOR

We are pressed to succeed everywhere we look, and this is a great thing. If you take some time to search on the Internet, in your local bookstore, or on Amazon, there are thousands of books and articles that will tell us how to be a success. It's the hopes and dreams of the world all rolled up into one. Feels good, doesn't it? How do you get your slice?

We can learn from those who have already succeeded, those that can only teach and those that don't even give their names. We are told that success brings with it all the trappings that you might want –

- The ability to live the life YOU want!
- Never to have to work for someone else again!
- Riches beyond your wildest dreams!
- The choice to go on vacation whenever you choose!

We are all attracted to words like these. For most people, it is a dream to be able to live a life like the one outlined above. We see people on MTV Cribs or read the glossy celebrity magazines and see that they are living the life of our dreams. Yes, let's read that again – our dreams.

YET, SUCCESS IS ONLY A FEW FAILURES AWAY

Success feels linear when you read about it. It feels like everyone who has become successful starts exactly where you are now and then moves closer to their dream life every day. We are told to think about growing our business or making a positive change in our life by taking it one step at a time. We are told that all of these steps add up to the destination we are targeting.

IT'S ALMOST AS IF WE AREN'T ALLOWED TO FAIL

Yes, I've said it. "Failure is not an option." We have heard that phrase so many times in our lives that it is almost impossible to remember where we first heard it and what it actually meant at the time.

- Little league coaches use it when they have a season-defining game they want to win.
- People use it at the gym when they want to push themselves further than ever before.
- School kids use it when they have a test that they think is important.

We start to think that no one who has ever amounted to anything could have failed at any stage of their life. The most successful people are seen as those that have "made it". Yet, we are never really shown the steps that they took to get to their place.

MESSAGE FROM THE AUTHOR

First and foremost, we don't actually know if they have reached a place in their lives in which they are happy. We just assume that they are where they want to be and got there by following a straight path that looked and smelled like success every single day.

Did you ever play the game when you were a kid where you hid something? The person who is looking for it was told that they were "warmer" or "colder" based on their movements. Most people think that is what success feels like. You feel warmer every day because you are closing in on the prize.

Let me tell you that the world doesn't work like that. If you map out success for people that you admire today, their route won't be a straight line between where you are now and where they have gotten to. The message here is that you shouldn't be afraid to get "colder" on some days. These are the days where you work out a route that just isn't going to work for you.

THIS IS YOU, IN REALITY, GETTING WARMER

The world isn't structured in a way where you start at A and wind up at Z, but don't sweat it. That's the fun part. The happiness is in the journey as much as the destination.

If you asked people to map out their line of success, it would look like a squiggly mess. There will be some movements towards their goal with some failures along the way. Some days will feel like progress while others will feel like a major setback. Don't kid yourself that success is a matter of joining the dots.

AND WHAT IS SUCCESS ANYWAY?

Does the store owner who has made it to four local stores feel just as successful as Warren Buffett? If he/she doesn't, then why not? The owner has made something from nothing – and then repeated that success three more times. That deserves a massive round of applause. If you know others in your circle of contacts that have achieved something like this then take the time now, yes right now, to congratulate them. Celebrating success is an important part of our path, as is embracing failure.

But don't think that opening four stores must become your own definition of success. That is up to you. Success is what we want it to be. Defining yourself by the standards or achievements of others does you no favors at all and won't lead to you actually FEELING successful.

Don't look to other people to set your standards. By all means, look to them for inspiration. This book will be filled with inspirational stories from many people who have gone on to success. What's the difference between this book and others you might find on the market?

I celebrate failure! Not in the sense that I am only looking for people who didn't make it. But in the sense that these are people who faced setbacks and were able to define their own ideal of what success looks and feels like before going on to achieve it.

MESSAGE FROM THE AUTHOR

But at the same time, don't limit yourself. If you want to be the next Jeff Bezos or Mark Zuckerberg, then go for it. Nobody else knows what you are capable of. Set your sights for what will define success for you.

Don't think that failure is the end. In the most real sense of it all, this is just the beginning. Failure doesn't close the wrong doors unless you allow it to. It closes the door that you don't want to travel through again. But it still leaves all of the other doors open. Think about the successes you have in your life so far. Think about how they measured up against your failures.

This book embraces the times where you just got something wrong – and then fixed it. There's no such thing as a complete failure. Just a little stumbling block on the road to greater success. Let's take a look at what this has meant to some people that you might not think ever suffered a failure.

FORWARD BY
AARON SHAFFER PSYD

The thought of failure can leave people feeling paralyzed and prevent them from going for their dreams. It can be especially difficult for those who have already achieved a great deal in academics, sports, or their career. Even though they have overcome challenges and setbacks in order to reach their achievements, when faced with new goals, the thought of failure can be frightening.

With 20 years as a coach to CEO's and athletes, I've learned to see failure differently. Over the course of a career that includes leadership and talent management roles at Motorola, ITT Industries, and Network Appliance, as well as consulting with Fortune 100 through start-ups, I've gotten to see the habits and attributes that create success, and those that hold people back, and the way in which an individual interprets failure and in turn his ability to bounce back quickly - is a key element to success.

Oftentimes, for the head of a successful company, an entrepreneur or a high-impact executive, failure is a strong motivator. In many cases, it's a fear of failure that encourages them to work harder, think deeper, and push their limits just a little bit more than others. It's that little bit that differentiates them from everyone else. For many, the thought of failure is a positive indicator that they're on the leading edge of what's possible. It's the advice of my early ski instructor who said, "If you don't occasionally

MESSAGE FROM THE AUTHOR

crash, you're not really trying hard enough." How will you know where your limits are unless you push a bit beyond them from time to time?

Patrick Williams and I first met when we were working with a start-up. It was a solid business idea, meeting the usual challenges of an entrepreneurial adventure in an emerging market. Patrick had a great reputation in the business, and we both found that many of our successes had roots in some form of failure — overtested limits, worst-case scenarios. My successes and failures had been largely in tech, and Patrick's in real estate development. We spent several lunches talking through what we'd seen, why things happened the way they did, and what the lessons were that we derived from these experiences.

Two themes began to emerge from those conversations. The first was that people who go big are willing to take big risks. This doesn't mean they're reckless or that they don't have a healthy fear of failure. More often, they realize that they are more likely to regret the chances they didn't take in life, than the chances they did take. It means, they recognize that playing it safe in every aspect of life limits your potential returns.

The second lesson from our experiences was that people who turn their insights into action are the ones who get the results they want. They are also more resilient and often outperform their peers. My guess is that many of us have a friend who has read all the best business books and has an ongoing self-help library, but none of the new information and knowledge seemed to improve their results in business or life. This is because they were more addicted to the process of development, than actually taking the actions required to get them to their desired goals.

Failure is often the point at which we learn and grow. It's the equivalent of the intense workout that breaks down the muscle, allowing it to rebuild itself so that the body comes back stronger. Failure can be the valuable lesson of what not to do, or to provide the moment of epiphany of what to do.

Failure is a lesson with feedback to show you what is effective and what is ineffective. The rewards of taking risks and overcoming your fear of failure is the freedom to pursue your passion and your dreams. If you don't embrace fear and failure, you become a prisoner of your fears and you inadvertently end up taking the biggest risk of all – the risk of not leading the life you were meant to live and sharing your unique gifts with the world.

PART 1

WHAT IS FAILING TO SUCCESS?

FAILURE IS NOT THE OPPOSITE OF SUCCESS, IT'S A PART OF IT!

PATRICK WILLIAMS

It is all well and good throwing a set of words around and expecting people to understand exactly what you mean. "Failing to success" could mean a lot of things to different people. I will define the phrase fully here, because we will rely on this definition throughout the rest of the book.

So, let's have a go at defining it:

- It is where you BOUNCE BACK from a massive drop to scale the heights again.

- It is where you SET YOUR OWN IDEALS in terms of success.

- It is where you DON'T LET SETBACKS STOP YOU from coming back at it the next day.

- It is where you DON'T LET OTHER PEOPLE'S DEFINITION OF SUCCESS define YOU.

Failure is often a necessary step toward success and the success lies in the journey of not giving up. A pivot is not giving up but realizing a different path to take.

You should be more fearful about not doing anything to begin with rather than the fear of failure. The future is one that you can shape as a driver, or one that you can experience as a passenger. I know which one I'd rather be!

The perfect time will never happen, so don't procrastinate because that is most often the trap that allows us not to make a decision.

I feel the best way to overcome the feeling of failure to succeed is persistence and endurance through the difficult time that will lead you closer to success. The only true failure is when you give up trying. The Rules of being Human:

Rule #1: You will learn lessons

Rule #2: There are no mistakes - only lessons

Rule #3: A lesson is repeated until it is learned

Rule #4: If you don't learn the easy lesson, they get harder.

Rule #5: You will know you have learned a lesson when your actions change.

What I have learned is that success is not a destination but instead the journey you take.

Failing to success means that you are not held back by inhibitions. If you only think about how to not fail, then the work that you do will be safe. It might not get you into any trouble, or lead to a loss of money, but it will never make you great at what you want to be great at – on your own terms.

> **"Success is not final; failure is not fatal: it is the courage to continue that counts."** — Winston S. Churchill

The greatest books are often those that are vastly different to everything that has been written before. Ditto the best movies, the best TV shows and the best music.

Why?

Because they offer something you can't get anywhere else. But the producers of this great music, this great fiction and those great visual treats have really gone out on a limb. They could have played it safe and delivered something that the market was expecting. They could have been mildly successful with it, but they were prepared to fail – and probably prepared to fail miserably.

Make this your mantra in life. As soon as you become afraid, you lose the power to shape the world. This is a wonderful power that has been bestowed on all of us. We have the choice of using this gift or wasting it. I know that you want to succeed. I'm here to tell you that you might fail along the way. Don't worry about this one little bit.

There are not enough people out there that are prepared to fail. They want to succeed instead.

> **"I have not failed. I've just found 10,000 ways that won't work."** — Thomas A. Edison

Failing isn't an intransigent thing. Failing once doesn't mean failing at everything for the rest of your life. The best football teams don't pack up and call it a day if they lose a game. They don't give up if they lose the first few games of the season. They keep working at what they believe in until they get it right. Teams lose their first game and still go on to win the Superbowl.

And it is the same in every part of your life. A failure to lose five pounds in weight this month doesn't mean that you will fail to lose it next month. You can, you will, you must.

But we don't seem to be able to apply this same logic to business. We either succeed or fail – the media won't let us think that there is any other outcome. Those who succeed walk away with all the plaudits, awards and money. Those that don't work their way to success end up on the scrapheap, don't they? Nope. They get up off their asses and make things happen. This book is filled with those stories. Read them and find your way.

> **"There is only one thing that makes a dream impossible to achieve: the fear of failure."**
> — Paulo Coelho, The Alchemist

Success is the end goal. But if we only want success for every small step along the way then that goal becomes ever farther in the distance. The journey along the way is all part of the fun! If you only achieve success, then your opportunities to learn disappear from view. You will never know how to put things right.

Small businesses are the perfect example of "failing to success." The survival rate for a small business starting out today is painfully low. There are so many barriers to success, such as:

- Cost to set up
- Customer loyalty
- Fighting against established players in the market
- Staff turnover
- Sentiment

This stacks the odds wildly against the start-up business. But they succeed all the time.

This feels like there is little chance that they can win, but they do. Finding that customer after customer doesn't want to deal with you can give you the impression that it is the end. Stopping is an option that soothes the aching soul. But it doesn't get the job done. You would be forgiven for throwing it all in and walking away. It is much safer to work for someone else instead. But billionaires across the globe faced the exact same challenges, dusted themselves off and kept on trucking.

> **"Failure is the condiment that gives success its flavor."** — Truman Capote

But if you roll with the punches then you can start to see the light at the end of the tunnel. The times when a boxer is pinned against the ropes and hanging on can just be the storm they must overcome before they find their feet in a fight. If they stay the distance, then there is always the chance that they land a punch that turns things around.

Your life is exactly the same. You don't put your head in the sand if you face a slight problem.

> **"Only those who dare to fail greatly can ever achieve greatly."** — Robert F. Kennedy

So, this book will look at the people who have fought back. It will look at the people who have dared to go out into the world and try to achieve something different, something extraordinary. It would be easy to Google people who had failed and succeeded, but that's not what we are trying to achieve here. That's for a blog post, not for a book.

The idea behind this book is that we look at the lessons to be learned from individual or collective failures that wound up in success. Businesses across the globe can learn from the failures of others. They say that you should learn from your mistakes. I say it is much easier (and far less costly) to learn from other people's mistakes.

There are so many diverse lessons to learn and take away for your life, that it would be amiss of me to gloss over them. Each chapter will marry a story from the world of failure, with something that you can take away and use in your personal life or business life.

We never stop learning. It is a lifelong thing. So, we will look together at all the ways that you can take a failure and move on or avoid one altogether.

> "Life is full of screwups. You're supposed to fail sometimes. It's a required part of the human existence." — Sarah Dessen, Along for the Ride

Don't ever be afraid of what life is about to throw at you. The way that you live for today cannot take into account every possible eventuality of tomorrow. You can only act on what you know, so let's make the best of what we have in front of us right now. If you try something and it doesn't work out, what's the worst that can happen?

- You waste some time.
- You lose some money.
- You close a door.

So what? There are so many other doors left for you. Failure doesn't cost you an arm or a loved one. Just pack up your belongings and start again.

We will look at the entrepreneurs who thought they had a great idea and then went bankrupt chasing it. They came back again with a refined version of the same idea and made millions.

We will look at the creative people who couldn't get others to share their vision. They kept on doing what made them happy and eventually their passion reached the entire world.

We will look at people who didn't have just one idea, but thousands. A creative mind and an appetite to make a difference in the lives of others is sometimes all it takes to create that one diamond among all of the cubic zirconia. But before we take a look at all of these weird and wonderful stories (and what they mean to you and your life) we have one question to consider.

"WHY FAIL TO SUCCESS?"

We will look at what that means in the next chapter. But first, let's look at a quote that is now well over a hundred years old, but is still just as relevant today when the 26th President of the United States delivered it:

> "It is not the critic who counts; not the man who points out how the strong man stumbles, or where the doer of deeds could have done them better. The credit belongs to the man who is actually in the arena, whose face is marred by dust and sweat and blood; who strives valiantly; who errs, who comes short again and again, because there is no effort without error and shortcoming; but who does actually strive to do the deeds; who knows great enthusiasms, the great devotions; who spends himself in a worthy cause; who at the best knows in the end the triumph of high achievement, and who at the worst, if he fails, at least fails while daring greatly, so that his place shall never be with those cold and timid souls who neither know victory nor defeat."

Stride into the rest of the book with these words ringing in your ears.

YOUR NEW MINDSET

So you can get started on the right foot going forward, just some of your FAILING TO SUCCESS attitudes and thoughts will include:

- You will be MORE FEARFUL about NOT starting (anything).
- You'll always know, the PERFECT TIME (to start anything) will

NEVER happen. The time to start (anything) is NOW.

- The only TRUE FAILURE is when you GIVE UP trying.
- SUCCESS is NOT A DESTINATION, but instead the journey you take, the lessons you learn
- Since so many others HAVE FAILED on their way to success, I will not think about failure as anything bad anymore. In fact, I will embrace it. "Bring it (fail) on," I will say.
- I'm going to be patient, stay the course, persevere, get up when I fall and give it my all ... all the way until I succeed.

PART 2

WHY FAIL TO SUCCESS?

SUCCESS IS THE ABILITY TO GO FROM FAILURE TO FAILURE WITHOUT ANY LOSS OF ENTHUSIASM OR MOTIVATION!

PATRICK WILLIAMS

On the face of it, this is a simple question. You could follow the path that so many others have trodden before. You could:

- Work hard at school so that you are in the best position for your exams.
- Pass all of these with flying colors so the options open to you are as wide as possible.
- Choose to go to a great school, maybe the Ivy League, and meet many other people who are similar to you.
- Study like mad to become the best you can be. In addition, join as many societies and teams as time allows to gain more influence.
- Get the best grades at the end of college life, so all the biggest companies in the country or the world are knocking on your door.
- Find a suitable company to work for.
- Keep your head down, play the corporate game and move up through the ranks.
- Become respected at what you do and generate great income from playing your role.
- Retire a wealthy person.

I'm not knocking this, or trying to make it sound easy, but from where we stand now, this feels a whole lot easier than failing. A steady job, a good income and a solid company. Who doesn't want all of that? What about fulfillment? Hmmm, that's not issued but earned, not a given but a challenge. It is built on the struggles of risk, failure, criticism, and overcoming difficult circumstances.

For most of us, life isn't the steady and smooth progression from childhood through school, family, work and life. We run into bumps, setbacks, which are often self-inflicted. Many struggle to get to where they are. Life doesn't always seem to follow the patterns as described above. Quite frankly, I wouldn't want it to. The highs and lows are what make things interesting. Failing to succeed is the risk that we all take when we do something we are passionate about – something we love.

Love itself is a similar thing. What if we tell someone we love them, and they don't reciprocate? How does that make us feel?

In our private life, we usually just go for it. We say those three little words and hope that the other person feels the same. But when it comes to business, we don't always have the same level of freedom.

This is even more so true if we own a business that is doing steadily well. We don't want to rock the boat. So, we drift along hoping that things will turn out right in the end. Even if we allow ourselves to define success, that's probably never going to feature in any definition of the word. Drifting is something that we think others do when we are moving slowly towards a goal.

We can all lose our way a little at times and wind up not moving very far. But moving in one direction or another – either failure or success – is actually far more productive than maintaining the status quo and hoping that everything will turn out okay in the end. Think about how this applies to your life right now.

What is it they say? If you are standing still, you are going backwards. In business, your competitors won't be standing still. They will be doing all they can to get ahead of you. You

PART 2 – WHY FAIL TO SUCCESS?

should be fighting tooth and nail to compete with them. You should be the one sticking out your neck.

The desire to move from where we are to somewhere else must be innate. Whether it comes natural or not, your actions should be fluid and natural. This means that you shouldn't have to second guess anything, per se. Sure, think things through some, plan things out some, but still ... GO FOR IT!

Check out the Internet. Most of the places we go are safe and familiar to us. But every now and again we come across something that intrigues us but scares us a little, too.

- Become a millionaire
- Win with every bet you place
- Quit your job in 30 days
- Lose weight in 2 weeks
- Reverse Type 2 diabetes
- Learn forex trading and make millions a trade

These all follow along the lines of the 'get rich quick' schemes that are advertised extensively on the Internet if you travel; to the places that are not familiar and comfortable. But they could just as easily be labelled 'get slim quick' or 'get well quick' schemes.

In essence, they are a shortcut. We like the idea because they promise to take the potential of failure away from us. We are told that these people have been through what we are going through. We are told that there is a painless solution. We are told that these are 'tried and tested' methods.

Look through these different sales pages, and you will find commonalities with all of them:

- They ask questions that all garner the same response
- They tell you about your problem
- They confirm how it can make you feel
- They offer a solution
- They tell you the solution works
- They provide testimonials that confirm it has worked for others
- They ask you to buy
- They usually pressure the sale by telling you that there is a limited supply, or the price will change soon

But the one thing that sits behind all of this is the chance to find the answer to your problem without the fear of failure. And guess what?

These schemes won't work for most people. There might be the odd person who signs up, follows it to the letter and makes a success of it. That's great. But if we are looking for a solution that doesn't include failure as an option, then we are not in the right frame of mind to make this a success.

If the only probability of failure is losing a few dollars (or a few hundred dollars with some of these schemes) and this is a very high probability, then we don't take the necessary steps to succeed. We're passing all of the risk on to someone else. We want their system to deliver us what we desire. There is no reason to be like that. You are a capable human being. You can make a success of whatever you want in life.

PART 2 – WHY FAIL TO SUCCESS?

Think about it.

It's like a child who is never told that their behavior is unacceptable. They push the boundaries every day. They know that there will be no repercussions for their actions. Our behavior when following a 'get X quick' scheme is the same. We will cheat a little on the calorie counting because we have a scheme that will look after us. We don't follow every step on the forex trading instructions because some look silly and others are far too complicated to follow every time. Once we start to mess with the system to our own ideals it stops working. We think that the safety net of 'never being able to fail' will always be there. That's still the same safe way of thinking. The safety net is an illusion. You might think you can see it; you might think it's just underneath you. It's not. You wouldn't want it to be.

If you are reading this book, then you will have heard of the carrot and the stick. It has long been seen as a poor way to manage people, but it is inherent in everything we do. The carrot is always seen as the way to move forward. People love the carrot. It provides the motivation to get up in the morning. It is a powerful tool. The stick is frowned upon. We are told that managers who regularly apply the stick are not very good at what they do. For this book, there are two major reasons that the stick is important:

1. We are looking at managing ourselves, not others ...

2. The stick is always there, whether we want it to be or not ...

Motivating yourself can be much more effective if we use the stick. It allows us to put that level of fear behind what we do. It allows us to think strategically about how to evade the impending failure that is always creeping up behind us.

Apple is a hugely successful business. But even as they launched their first iPhone, they were planning the next. They knew that failure was stalking them. They knew that the rest of the telecom market would digest what they had produced and then deliver their own version. They knew that failure was a reality if they didn't keep their game up.

And for you, failure is always an option. A large business such as Apple might have a couple of failed products in them. They can absorb this. How many failures can you absorb? If you put $5 on every 'get rich quick' scheme you found on the Internet, then you would lose millions in a short space of time. So, failure is always there at the back of our mind as a motivation to learn more, do things better and improve. There is always a stick. It might be bankruptcy. It might be losing your home.

So, with this in mind, you should embrace the option of failure. It allows us to stay alert and learn the lessons of past failures. It is the lifeblood of what we are put on this earth for. Why fail to success? Why do things any other way?
Can you learn from failure?

Our brain is configured in a particular way. We have arrived here today as a result of the experiences and decisions that our ancestors made in the past. One of the built-in triggers is that we learn things. If one of our family members years ago was seriously hurt by something, they steered clear of it. We act in the same way today. If we hear of an airplane crash, there is a little voice inside our heads saying, "don't get on a plane." Statistically, the chances of dying in a plane crash haven't changed by that one event. But the trigger in our mind highlights the potential danger.

We get better at things because we learn. We learn that doing something that ends in failure is an act that we should avoid the next time. Our innate sense of survival can get in the way of our desire to learn from failure, or, at least, it can if we let it.

Greg Dickerson is a very great and successful guy. He has been involved in the real estate market for some time. Obviously, every purchase hasn't ended in unqualified success. There are some investments you make that will just bomb. That's the nature of what you do. He hasn't let failure get in the way of future success.

We have to break things down into single events, rather than seeing it as part of a pattern. For example, if you buy one property in a certain part of town for the wrong price and actually lose money on it, the temptation would be to avoid that part of town in the future. But it wasn't the part of town that caused the issue. It was the price you negotiated. The lesson is to negotiate better in the future. We can easily slip into the thinking that the lesson is to never invest our money again. Nothing ventured, nothing gained is the phrase. But we end up thinking nothing ventured, everything saved. We can't be like this if success is the final destination.

Greg Dickerson doesn't let these decisions get in the way of making the next one. That would be a crazy way to operate as someone who invests. When a person fails that is a single event and you learn from it and adjust and overcome. Failure is a frame of mind and how a person thinks and if they wallow in it, they will never try it again.

PONDER THIS

When endeavouring on any entrepreneurial project or investment, always assess your risk. It's exciting to look at the opportunities and rewards that make taking the risk look sexy and appealing. These are the things that get you out of bed every morning feeling excited and motivated to work.

What about the risks that come with it? These are the things that keep you up at night, worried and unable to sleep. However, if you go into each business endeavour with a clear road map that also takes into account the real risk involved, when you experience the inevitable losses and failures that come with taking risks, it won't be something that discourages you from ever trying again.

It's important to take calculated risks and to honestly assess what you can afford to lose. You need to take a holistic approach to running a business and that means assessing the business as well as taking personal inventory of your own life and values. Ask yourself these questions:

- What are your needs and what are your wants?

- How much money do you need every month to meet your needs and how long of a financial cushion do you have to sustain you?

- Are you willing to risk your health for your business? If not, how much sleep and exercise do you need to maintain your health? What will you do to keep your stress levels in check? Meditation? Walks in nature? How will you ensure that you maintain a healthy diet?

- What about your relationships with your family and friends? What is that worth to you and how much time and energy do you plan to dedicate to these relationships?

- Is there something you would have rather been doing if you hadn't pursued your vision?

When you answer all of these questions for yourself, then you are able to assess how much time and money you are able and willing to risk. This enables you to pursue your dreams with a passion, knowing that if you fail, you know that it was still worth the blood, sweat and tears.

Taking risks isn't about jumping off of a cliff and hoping for the best. You need to take calculated risks and know that failure is not only a possibility, but a probability on the road to success.

Once you take an honest look at everything you have to lose by going for your dream, and you accept the risk, you are now free to take the steps towards achieving your goals. This freedom gives you confidence, and this confidence is felt by everyone you interact with. It draws people to you who want to help you achieve your goals and increases your chances for success.

PART 3

BELIEVE IN YOURSELF

BELIEVE IN YOURSELF! YOU'RE ALREADY UNSTOPPABLE!

PATRICK WILLIAMS

PART 3 – BELIEVE IN YOURSELF

Taking that first step on the road toward your success can be the most difficult. Inevitably, you'll be met with two divergent roads. The 'easy' road naturally fits into your daily stride pattern. Ideas flow and opportunities come easily. It feels right and the other roads feel big and sometimes feel impossible. You're often frustrated and feel more like a failure than a success. Ultimately, you may think you're heading in the wrong direction.

If you know where you want to be, then the easy road always feels like it is the best route. In many cases, it feels like it is the only route that you should take. Deviation from this feels like a betrayal. It feels like you have lost sight of your goal and are meandering. Don't fall into this trap.

You are not in control. None of us are in control of the process. The bigness of one road is as important as the ease of another.

Playing chess would be much easier if you played for both sides. It would mean that you could open up spaces and come to checkmate in no time at all. The game of chess is not like that – nor is the world. Some of your moves are designed to achieve something, while others may lead you down a blind alley. They might lead you to a crushing defeat, but the thing about chess is, the more you play it, the better you become.

It is the same with life. The more times you go through the front door every morning and try to be successful, the more likely you are to achieve that in the end. Walk out of that door with a huge smile on your face, knowing that you could fail at any minute and knowing that failing doesn't matter.

We must believe that the actions we are taking will lead to our final goal. If we don't have the courage in our convictions, then we will experience more defeats than wins.

The difference between a successful business and one that has failed is often about far more than whether they had the right products or if they found a market for their goods. It is often about defining what they do in terms of their path to success. Let me explain.

Making decisions is all a part of business. Even deciding to not make a decision is a decision in itself. So, businesses are faced with scores of decisions every day. If these are made on a case by case basis by having a gut feeling, then they are less likely to succeed. Why? Because they are not part of an overall strategy that is designed to deliver success.

This can easily lead to a business failure.

> **"My past is everything I failed to be."**
> — Fernando Pessoa

The successful business is able to make decisions that fit into a strategy. They can give their team members a culture, a message and then let them decide on how their decisions fit into this.

These businesses have a vision. They know where they want to be, and to back this up, they believe in themselves. They believe in themselves so much that they allow all of their decisions to be centered in this vision, and it really works. Oh, it really works!

You see, the vision that you have should define what you do. It is taking you along a path and without a crystal ball. You don't really know whether this path leads you to success or to failure. But even if there are setbacks on the way, even if it all starts to fall apart, then you will have your ideas, your beliefs and the experience of failure to spur you on to the next level. Let's take a look at someone who has been through a similar experience. Peer pressure can have a massive impact on this. We all want others to tell us how great we are. If someone is letting us know we are brilliant, then we feel validated. Travis Chappell

PART 3 – BELIEVE IN YOURSELF

is a real estate investor and network building podcaster, and he sees the potential issues in always looking to your peers for the validation that makes you feel like you are on the right track. If we all follow the same path as those around us, then we wind up being the same person, essentially.

Peer pressure comes into play when we are young and stays with us our whole life. We will look in more detail later in the book at the education system and the role it has to play in failure. But for now, let's consider the fact that we are all pushed to conform from an early age. This means we stop taking the risks that can lead to innovative thinking.

Winning is when you lose at something because you have learned valuable lessons. It is as simple as that.

Travis Chappell takes up the rein, "Changing your environment is important. You need to be around positive like-minded people. Example being around other entrepreneurs who have failed it's not a big thing because it's part of the journey and they say just get back on the horse and there is no shame. People who have jobs tend to be more negative about failing and tend to say that's why they play it safe and have jobs."

With that in mind, the next chapter looks at entrepreneurs.

But first, let's take a look at what might happen if you don't believe in yourself. Holly Pasut was a real estate professional back in the day. It comes across that she didn't believe in herself. She took shortcuts and this landed her in a whole heap of trouble. Indeed, so much trouble that she ended up in prison for two years for mortgage fraud.

The time in prison gave Holly time to reflect on her life and how she ended up there. Rather than going for self-pity, Holly looked at how she could bounce back. She wasn't going to let that failure define her.

She really thought about what she wanted to become and her life legacy. It wasn't about money or libraries being donated in her name. She wanted her legacy to be her character and how she lived her life and how she could pass that onto her children. Failing is about learning and it is a part of life. But what you do about those life events that happen to you is what defines you. Holly believes that things will always happen in life. Some we can't control. What matters is how we react to things, which is 90% of what happens in life.

TAKE ACTION ON THIS

A step you can take to change how you see failure, is recognize how failure has impacted you. The lessons you learned from your mistakes contribute to how you will do things differently going forward.

Then determine what part of the failure were circumstances that were beyond your control. Accept that with every business there are many unforeseeable variables that provide us with challenges, which we can turn into opportunities if we are able to reframe the "problems" and find creative solutions.

Every failure is just telling you what direction not to go in, so that you can course correct and discover your path to success.

PART 4

TAKE ACTION!

ACTION, NOT WORDS WILL GET YOU WHERE YOU WANT TO GO!

PATRICK WILLIAMS

PART 4 – TAKE ACTION!

To go from idea to reality often requires taking bold decisions, opting to take a risk, or making a personal change. I can't tell you how many people I know have captured the academic essence of leadership, innovation and entrepreneurship, but haven't turned it into action.

I can say the same thing about most of the business books that promise a guided path to personal and professional success. From execution, leadership to management, the shelves are lined with actionless books that describe a direction, without actual steps that take action.

For sure action often leads to failure but without you actually moving forward you'll never get to where you want to go. So, in the most simple of terms:

TAKE ACTION NOW, NOT TOMORROW & LIFE WILL START MOVING FORWARD IN THE DIRECTION YOU WANT!

PART 5

ENTREPRENEURS

ISN'T IT TIME YOU STARTED WORKING FOR YOU?

PATRICK WILLIAMS

PART 5 – ENTREPRENEURS

We read about it all the time. We hear about how someone comes up with an idea in their bedroom or at work and turns it into a billion-dollar business. The press tells us it's an overnight success story. We all look on with wide eyes and hope that we can come up with an idea just like this. We hope that we can come up with a similar idea and change our world. This hope is what makes the world go around and fills us with joy and happiness.

The idea of the overnight millionaire or billionaire is something that appeals to our sense of winning. We want to win – and we are prepared to put in the hard work if we know there is success at the end of the line. But when we scour the Internet and read that others are successful from little or no effort, we pre-condition our brain to want the same. Why would we work hard when there is the potential for riches with little or no effort? But the press was not there when these entrepreneurs first had the idea. They were not there when the entrepreneurs were scratching around for funding. They were not there when the business founders thought about throwing it all in because it was causing them sleepless nights and grey hair.

We all want a piece of the good life and a slice of pie that takes no effort at all. You could win the lottery and win big or a jackpot that is worth hundreds of millions. But even that takes the effort of going to the store, waiting in line and buying a ticket. There is a small amount of effort in return for a potential big prize, but the odds are stacked against you.

But what if you could exchange hard work for a prize? Would you still enter? If the success wasn't guaranteed – would you still enter then?

That's life.

Take Manpreet Singh, an entrepreneur that was living the good life, working for someone else with a steady income and the trappings of success in the corporate world. Manpreet launched TalkLocal.com, a tech start-up that he has grown from two to more than 50 employees.

He decided that there must be something better than the life he was living. It was a stressful thing to consider walking away from the comfort and going on a journey that could lead to failure. He took the time to plan and prepare for his life away from his job and strike out on his own. It was a huge risk. The life he had worked hard to build and his employer gave him a paycheck in return every month in exchange for his time. You can just imagine how scary it might have been for anyone to launch out on their own under such circumstances as he had.

That's quite a leap of faith for most people. Taking away the safety net of pay in exchange for attendance can send some people into a tailspin. The pressure of providing for themselves, and, possibly a family, can stop you from functioning properly.

This is the fear of failure. We do not define ourselves by the success or failure of our decisions. That's the cop out and if we look back over the last 5, 10, or 20 twenty years of our life we will notice that we are defined by our decisions. The decisions are always the fork in the road.

It's the work we put in after the decision that determines whether it was successful or not.

Manpreet had built up his business without a fear of failure. Instead of the "what if it goes wrong?" attitude, we should all look at what can go right, and not dreams of a distant future where we are relaxing on a desert island with investments worth billions. That isn't success for most.

PART 5 – ENTREPRENEURS

The safety net has blinded us. We don't define what we are by what we do.

Success for many is a life where you can:

- Get up every day and do something you love
- Learn all the time to develop your skills and ability
- Grow as a person more than as an employee
- Follow your passions in life

There are no better opportunities than these. Note that none of these feature the word "money". None of these dreams look at the safety net of being paid every month by someone else. People don't sit on their death bed wishing they had made more money. They sit there looking back at memories. That's what all of the above are – memories.

Now consider what might stop you from achieving your goals or dreams. There will be obstacles in the way of success or progress. These stumbling blocks can slow you down in reality.

"Face your fears, but only with a well-armed army and a deep arsenal to ensure that they shrink in comparison to your preparedness and competence."

The challenges that you face in business are often not the ones that you mulled over before beginning. Ask any entrepreneur what their biggest challenge has been, and it is hardly ever what they thought it would be before the business launched. So, we stress over issues that don't end up being an issue. We stop being the entrepreneur because of perceived problems. We let our fears rule our spirit of adventure. Don't do that and open your wings so you can soar!

Manpreet Singh was living the life that many of us face today. He was living a comfortable existence. But he looked failure in the eye and decided that he was going to test himself. The comfort zone is probably a good place to be in when working for someone else. You might get your best work done if you feel safe and happy. You fit into the machine and deliver exactly what is expected of you.

But in your own business, you need to stay out of your comfort zone. Being comfortable allows your competitors to pass you by. It means you don't make your product or service better all the time. It stops you from innovating.

These are all the places that the entrepreneur does not want to be.

In fact, it is probably the difference between the company owner and the employee. The owner has taken risks, stays outside of their comfort zone and pushes forward. The employee benefits from this, but never truly experiences what it is like to be that free. You should look to freedom in everything you do.

TalkLocal.com connects professionals with people that need the service of a professional service provider. It sounds so simple, but what is the number one hassle associated with finding a service professional? It's making all the calls and finding the right person. TalkLocal.com does all of that. FOR FREE!

The risk with this business is that if talklocal.com didn't get the right professionals on board, they could end up with a service where professionals didn't want to pay for their referrals, or a business where a few poor reviews could lead to a lack of trust in the service.

The risk is pretty evident. Manpreet could have walked away from a comfortable life into a nightmare business. But that didn't stop him from innovating. He had that much faith in his business that he was prepared to take that leap of faith.

And being scared about the potential outcome can be a positive factor – if you channel it into the right actions. Always looking over your shoulder at the next potential failure is tough. It drains energy and directs all the effort of your business in the wrong direction. Fighting fires becomes a habit if you allow it.

Looking at the future of the business puts a different outlook on everything. It's like the decision a writer makes in how to position their characters. They set up a hero and often a bad guy as well as peripheral characters. You feel for the hero and it's deliberate to despise the villain.

In your business, you set the same tone with your focus. If it is on making things better, then you start to look away from failure and towards success. Your mindset is a major factor in the potential success of your idea going from inception to reality.

And we are back full circle to the "overnight success" entrepreneurs that we started the chapter with. They didn't do all of this overnight. They worked at their idea and nurtured it. The alternative was to discard it as "too risky" or "bound to fail". Think about all of the great ideas that were never brought into reality because of the potential for failure.

I'm willing to bet that there was someone out there who had a similar idea to iTunes but thought it wouldn't work. There must be plenty of investors who turned down Jeff Bezos because Amazon looked like a financial basket case.

That's the difference between the entrepreneur that makes it, and the ones that fall short.

Manpreet could have stayed in his high-paying job and been

comfortable for life. But comfortable doesn't often fire your imagination. *TalkLocal.com* did and still does.

WHAT HAVE WE LEARNED SO FAR?

We now recognize that failure and setbacks are part of the process. We've learned how to reframe failures as opportunities, and we've calculated our risks so that we are free to pursue our ideas with the knowledge and peace of mind that we can afford to have failures.

Now it's time to focus on the possibilities and the direction we want to go. When I was doing my motorcycle license training, the first thing we learned is that if we focus our eyes on what we don't want to hit, that's the direction the motorcycle is going to go and we're going to end up crashing.

You've done your risk assessment; you no longer need to focus on all the things that could go wrong. This wastes time and energy and distracts from the goal.

An entrepreneur needs to have tunnel vision and to stay focused on where he/she's going. Have a business plan that outlines where you're going and how you're going to get there. There will be setbacks, detours and the destination may even change, but the focus is always on where you want to go.

Stay positive and take time to celebrate the small achievements along the way. This keeps you and your team motivated and keeps the momentum and focus on the goal.

> "There is only one thing that makes a dream impossible to achieve: the fear of failure."
> — Paulo Coelho, The Alchemist

PART 6

YOU ARE YOUR ART

THERE'S BEAUTY IN ART, EVEN WHEN IT'S NOT UNDERSTOOD

PATRICK WILLIAMS

PART 6 – YOU ARE YOUR ART

Fiction is rife with stories of failure turned into success. A quick Internet search will show you scores of works of fiction that were deemed "not good enough" by publishing houses. Dr Seuss is a national institution. His works are loved by kids all over America and the rest of the world. Recent years have seen many of his ideas adapted into movies. It looks and feels like we have always loved the crazy world of Dr Seuss.

The world of publishing is a strange thing. Publishing houses often lament the fact that they are not shown anything different. If there is a crime thriller at the top of the bestseller list, then they are inundated with more crime fiction. They reject millions of manuscripts every year because they don't want to put out more of the same. But, if they are presented with something completely different, then they don't know what to do with it. They get what they asked for, but don't quite know how to market it, develop it and get the sales they want from a book that is "different!"

And that's exactly what the works of Dr Seuss were. You will be forgiven for thinking that his work is something that you can find in many other authors and illustrators. But that wasn't the case when he first started writing. His books were imaginative and ground-breaking. The publishing houses had no idea what to do with them.

He was turned down by no less than 27 publishers. Yes, you read that correctly. Dr Seuss, the national institution, was turned away from more than two dozen publishers. Why? Because they didn't have a clue what to do with his work. It was too different for their compartmentalized business. He produced his best work and went through all the right channels. He was rejected every time so how do you think that made him feel?

The first book was called *"And to Think I Saw it on Mulberry Street"* and the story goes that he decided after walking away from the 27th rejection that he would burn the book. It hadn't been a success and he was heading home to end the cycle of hope and rejection regarding the book.

Even the most talented people can feel desolate in the face of multiple rejections. It is fair to say that he had lost faith in his work.

On the way home, he bumped into an old acquaintance who asked him what he was carrying. Legend has it that Seuss (real name Theodor Geisel) replied that it was a manuscript he was taking home to burn. The acquaintance invited Geisel up to his office, introduced him to his publisher and they bought the rights to the book.

Since, Geisel has sold over 600 million books. In a famous quote, he states that if he had been walking along the opposite side of the street that day, then he would have been in the dry cleaning business instead.

And the world would have lost a great author.

This goes to show the power of the partner. Some industries are notoriously difficult to get into. I went to a talk put on by the publishing industry a few months back.

The first person to speak was a literary agent who said he gets around 3,500 submissions per year and takes on 2 of them.

Later in the day, a representative of a publishing house spoke about the fact that she gets around 2,500 submissions from literary agents each year (they don't accept unsolicited submissions) and takes on 2 of these. Let's do the math:

You have a 2 in 3,500 chance to be selected by a literary agent. If you make past the literary agent then you have a 2 in 2,500 chance to actually get your book chosen by a publisher.

The overall odds?

Based on those numbers you have a very slim chance in having your book published.

Does that mean you should pack up your stuff and walk away? Theodor Geisel nearly did. If he only made it by the skin of his teeth, then what chance do the rest of us have?

Did you notice the turning point in Geisel's story? It was when he got together with someone who championed his work. It didn't take long, but the old acquaintance could see something in the book – and the author.

Ever heard the story of The Beatles being rejected by Decca Records. They auditioned and were told that they didn't have a future in music.

They didn't find someone who believed in them. At first, anyway...

Even the talented author and illustrator Theodor Geisel needed someone who believed in him. Otherwise he was going home to burn the book that started the empire.

Finding an advocate that will speak up for you wasn't easy in those days. The connections were mainly local and very parochial. Indeed, The Beatles were turned down by Decca who concentrated on a group that not many have heard of but were local to the Decca office. They felt they could offer Brian Poole and the Tremeloes better support. I told you that you would have never heard of them!

We can now see the benefit of looking for the right partner or partners to support your work. It can transform the way you are received.

Luckily for The Beatles, they had Brian Epstein in their corner who believed wholeheartedly in what they were capable of. He pushed them towards other record labels, and they went on to worldwide fame and millions of records sold. This isn't just relevant in the creative industries. In the end, you find that people who shout loudly about your product do more for your sales than all of your marketing put together.

So, what would Geisel have done differently in today's market? Well, the rise of self-publishing may well have meant that he would publish the book without the need of a publisher to get his stories and ideas out there. His book would have appeared on Amazon Kindle and started its journey that way. Something as ground-breaking and high quality as this would probably have found the right audience, with word of mouth.

And your route to market isn't necessarily the same one that everyone else is taking. The world is filled with innovative companies that have disrupted the ideas of the past.

Without innovators we wouldn't have Uber, Airbnb or Amazon. They didn't want to follow the market. If they did:

- Jeff Bezos would have a chain of bookstores.
- Uber would be another taxi company.
- Airbnb would have scaled slowly because property is expensive to purchase.

Think about how your market can and will react to your product or service. Think about the diverse ways you can deliver to your customers.

Before he died, Prince gave away an album free of charge. Think about this, free music is something the industry had been fighting for years.

Why did he do this?

Because he used it as a promo to sell concert tickets. He sold out more shows in seconds all based on people listening to his new music for free. You can find the right market if you get the support and find a route. It doesn't have to be the traditional route, or the path always traveled to work.

And all of these strategies fit perfectly into the character we will explore in the next chapter.

FIND YOUR SUPPORT (PERSON)

You believe in your idea and that's why you're on this path, but sometimes it can be disheartening to receive multiple rejections from editors, VC's or potential customers. The world hasn't caught up to your ideas, but you know that you have something special to offer.

Find someone who believes in you and your idea. This can be a family member or a business colleague who can help you get through the tough times that create self doubt in even the best of us.

This doesn't mean that you surround yourself with "yes" people who blindly encourage and support you. Those who truly support you will want to challenge you with different ideas, and this is exactly the kind of people you need. You want to create an environment where your colleagues feel comfortable thinking outside of the box and looking at the business in new directions. You want to foster innovative thinking in everyone in the company such that everyone is also working to their highest ability.

The important thing is to know the difference between someone who can think critically and ask the tough questions, versus someone who is negative. It's very important that you only share your ideas with those who support you and believe in you. If you know that there are people in your life who will be negative, then refrain from talking with them about your goals. This will only bring you down and detract from your mission.

"When you possess great treasures within you, and you try to tell others of them, seldom are you believed."
— Paulo Coelho, The Alchemist

PART 7

THE FALL & RISE OF AMAZON & JEFF BEZOS

DETERMINATION, THROUGH FAILURES, LEADS TO SUCCESS

PATRICK WILLIAMS

PART 7 – THE FALL AND RISE OF AMAZON AND JEFF BEZOS

A book about *Failing To Success* wouldn't be the same without a chapter about the phenomenon that is Jeff Bezos. I have named this chapter the 'Fall and Rise' because for years the world was told that Amazon was heading for failure. It was the most written about business in the early years of this millennium and all of the press was bad. They had losses year after year. They looked like they would never turn a profit. We were told they were going to be the biggest failure of the dotcom age, and let's be clear, there were some big failures in the dotcom age!

With all of this pressure and negativity, you would have forgiven Bezos for packing it all in and walking away. He watched other entrepreneurs lose everything they had left, right and center as their ideas didn't gain traction. This was an age where a bubble grew up around the new industries of the early 2000's. The stock market loved them – to a point. Shares rose and rose as backers could see the potential for these fledgling companies, and then as they failed to turn a profit, the investment community turned their back on these businesses in droves. Share prices collapsed, and companies went under.

As the bigger names came under pressure, the scrutiny on Amazon intensified. The word on the street was that they couldn't survive. They were mocked in some quarters as an "emperor's new clothes" business. Once someone actually pointed out that they had nothing, it was all supposed to fall apart at their feet. Jeff Bezos summed it up in an interview:

> "People predicted our demise for so long we did develop thick skin. Invention requires a long-term willingness to be misunderstood. You do something that you genuinely believe in. Well-meaning people may criticize that effort. If they are not right, then you need to have that long-term willingness to be misunderstood."

They could have easily let this criticism hit them hard. They could have called it a day right there and then. But Amazon didn't. They still didn't turn a profit but, by hook or by crook, they stayed afloat. People were still using the platform in big numbers. The revenues were good, but the elusive profit looked a million miles away.

The first lesson for Jeff Bezos was that if an idea was something that he believed in wholeheartedly, then he needed to stick to it. The failure of others around him was their own business. The lack of short-term success in his own business was something he felt he could make right over time.

With some shocking losses, it would have been safe to walk away. He could have gone the same route as many other start-up entrepreneurs at the time and declared bankruptcy before starting over again.

The system in the U.S. is perfect to wash away past failures and begin again. This isn't a system that is repeated the world over. In some parts of the developed world, bankruptcy can finish you off, or at the very least slow you to a halt for at least six years.

So, with the potential to wash away his financial sins and start again, why didn't Bezos take this easy route? Mounting losses would have crippled the company and him. It goes back to whole-heartedly believing in what you do.

He may not have seen the global domination that he has now, but he did have a strong vision of how he was going to make this company a success. While he was at it, he would prove the doubters wrong. Doubters can affect you in one of two ways:

1. Make you more determined to succeed

2. Multiply the doubts you already have

We all walk around with doubts in our head every day of the week. We wonder if we can make a success of any particular project at any given time. We don't know what the outcome will be. It makes the whole thing exciting, but adds an element of fear at the same time. That's before we even share this idea with anyone else in the world. Giving an idea the light of day can help us to test whether our doubts were real or whether they were something we can overcome.

This idea might be as small as a blog or as big as making a change at work. Now put yourself in the shoes of the early millennium Jeff Bezos. Every move he made was analyzed and scrutinized. He couldn't make a decision or change without the media pulling it apart. The doubts he had would have been multiplied many times over if he didn't believe totally in Amazon.

He was able to block all of this out and believe even more strongly in Amazon. He was able to strengthen his resolve to get things right in spite of the doubters – or possibly because of them.

This carries to you and your business. Don't shut your ears to any feedback you are receiving, but make sure you have that strong core belief in what you do. There will be bumps along the road, and you will make adjustments, but the end result will be the one that you shape – not the views of other people. What is the common thread that runs through so many successful companies? It isn't that they hit the spot at the right time, or that they are backed by big money.

All of the influential people in these businesses are incredibly passionate about what they do. I assume that if you are running your own business, as many of the readers of this book will be, then it is something you care deeply about. If you don't, then your customers can see through this. The passion that you bring to your business every day:

- Inspires the people who work for you
- Makes meaningful connections to suppliers
- Is infectious to your customers

The business world is changing. There is so much competition for your product or service that you don't stand a chance unless you have that passion. Others will eat you for breakfast. Jeff Bezos started something that he was passionate about. He wanted to make a wide-ranging retailer that could provide a better service than what people could get offline. Now, that's a hugely difficult task to achieve. Offline, you can get face-to-face service, staff members that get to know you and the convenience of being close to home or work.

How did he go about beating this? His greatest asset became the customers that were not drawn to anything other than this company that wanted to make their life and service experience better.

Forget all the lower prices, one-day deliveries and other gimmicks that have been copied by online retailers the world over. That all paled into insignificance against the passion. Here is what Jeff has to say about it:

> "Make sure that you are focused on something you are passionate about. The early Internet companies were started and focused on something that they thought was very interesting. I like the underdog years. When all of the people we hired, their parents told them they were crazy. You can't follow the fashion when you have a start-up company – or anything in life. Stand there and let the wave catch you."

And the underdog mentality is a persuasive one for the kind of people Bezos was looking to recruit – the millennial generation. They are now edging the Baby Boomers out of the workplace and taking a foothold in shaping the future.

Millennials don't want to work in a boring, staid environment where they clock in and out in return for a paycheck. They want someone who will motivate and inspire them. They want an employer who believes in what they believe in. Guess what? It isn't just employees of Amazon that feel like this. Their customers want the same.

They want to buy from a retailer that feels what they feel, that experiences the world in the same way they do. Amazon has been just that.

For Bezos and Amazon, at the core of all this success is … FAILURE. It is never far away in retail. Jeff Bezos is one of the few entrepreneurs that is willing to take a risk and embrace failure as part of the process:

> **"I've made billions of dollars of failures at Amazon.com. Literally billions of dollars of failures. It's easy to have ideas. It is very hard to turn an idea into a successful product. Do something you are passionate about."**

So, with making billions of dollars of failures, how does he sleep at night? None of us have anywhere near this amount of money to throw away on failure. We look after every penny in our business, because it is important. It's not just important – it is vital to our success. We know that every penny we stop from going to waste will instead end up in the profit column on our balance sheet.

If we understand the overall vision, then we can make mistakes – as long as we learn from them. It is implied in the quote above because we know it is an outrageously successful businessman speaking. We know that when he states he made billions of dollars of failures, that these were part of a long-term story that winds up with him being one of the richest people in the entire world.

So, what is your long-term story? Can we look back on our mistakes with the same kind of indifference that Jeff Bezos does? Well, we can't look back on mistakes if we don't allow ourselves to go out there and make them. Remember that not making a decision is a choice. If we stand still, the market overtakes us, and we are history.

So, don't be afraid to make mistakes. Of course, we don't want to end up in the same situation as the dotcom companies that failed, but most of those founders got up and started again. They founded new businesses and went from one failure to another success. Sometimes with other failures in between. There is only one go at this thing called life. You don't want to slip off this mortal coil with the potential of being another Jeff Bezos and think that we didn't give it our best shot.

BE "SERVICE" FOCUSED (TO OTHERS)

Stay focused on your long-term vision and this will make the failures and setbacks seem insignificant. Building a successful company isn't a quick sprint, it's a long marathon with many steps along the way that require endurance.

When you believe in what you are doing, and you see the difference it will make in the lives of others, this makes the journey worthwhile.

It's about being of service to the world. It's not about what you're going to get, but about what you're going to provide for others. Employees and customers are drawn to companies that align with a cause that brings meaning and purpose to their lives and this is what drives productivity.

PART 8

THE AMAZING RACE & FACING ADVERSITY ON TV

ADVERSITY CAN YIELD FAILURE OR SUCCESS. IT'S YOUR CHOICE!

PATRICK WILLIAMS

PART 8 – THE AMAZING RACE & FACING ADVERSITY ON TV

Throughout our lives, most anyone who is seeking to accomplish a particular goal will face adversity of some kind. The average person will fail in their own time, in their own place and at their own pace.

We have already seen the public scrutiny that Jeff Bezos has been through in his life. But he always had that private space at home to walk away from the shining light of publicity to be himself. Television doesn't allow for the same level of privacy, particularly when it's a television realty show.

Once you sign up for a reality TV show, you are in a position where you are at the mercy of the producers and editors. How easy do you think it would be to fail to success there?

Joyce was a contestant on the popular show, Amazing Race and her story shows that even when your failures are particularly public, you can still fail to success.

One of the most memorable challenges on the show was when a team would come in last place, which often means that they were eliminated.

But in this instance, the team lost everything they gained during the previous shows in the series. They lost all their clothes, money and food. All that was left was a clear plastic bag with passports and medicine inside. The next challenge required the team to build a raft in the mud. Their clothes got muddy in the process. The next location was over two hours away from the raft building area so they had to hussle.

Joyce said, "You need the kindness of other people to help you succeed," as part of the realization that they were not going to achieve their goals by might and determination alone.

Sometimes you need to stop, take a step back and see how the road curves before moving to the next step.

The contestants were in a position where they had to improvise. The failure of one task was leading towards the failure of the next. Something had to break the cycle of failure, and this is the way it is in business. It would be easy to see one failure and assume that it would prompt a succession of more failures. But coming to grips with the task at hand and changing the cycle is what all strong and successful entrepreneurs do. The contestants spent their time begging for money in order to get to the next task and turn a potential second failure around.

"It was the most humbling and humiliating thing I have ever done," said Joyce as she explained that part of the series. She and her team could have just walked away from the show at that point. But they wouldn't let one failure define their route to success for the rest of the series.

The way that this task went, showed in clear focus the way that failure doesn't mean the end of the road. Many business owners hit a place where they feel they can go no further and then drop everything. The journey of any one business or person never follows in a straight line from where they are now to the place they want to be.

Joyce and her teammate sat on the street begging after one small failure set them off track. We judge others in our personal and business life by the way they look or the situation they are in, but we have no idea about the story that lead them to the place they are in today. It opens our eyes to how success and failure can define us. "I'll never judge people who are on the streets because I don't know how they got there. It was definitely the most memorable event of the show," Joyce explained.

From that challenge, Joyce learned to be humble about her

PART 8 – THE AMAZING RACE & FACING ADVERSITY ON TV

talents and successes. She showed her vulnerability, and this opened up her situation and character to others. Showing the world that you need a little help from time to time doesn't have to be a sign of weakness. It is just a sign of your current state. This whole book talks about failing to success – so we shouldn't be surprised that there are the odd failures along the way. We should expect them to happen every now and again and just roll with them. Say thank you for the lessons learned. Keeping absolute control of every situation in every way can only lead to two things:

1. That you never take any risks
2. That you end up chasing your tail

Neither of these are great places to be in. Never taking a risk means that you don't push yourself and never learn. Having just about everything taken from them on The Amazing Race could have been the end of the road as far as the show was concerned for Joyce and her team. The risk was to get back up and try to make the next task work in the face of pretty stacked odds, and going way out of their comfort zone was obviously the only way they could move forward in any way at all.

Chasing your tail trying to make sure that nothing is outside your limits might work if you have a small business that doesn't make a lot of money or have a lot of facets, but that's probably not what you have got into business for. As you grow, then you need to let go of a few things. If you have employees, then you need to train, coach, supervise, and then trust them to do the job you hired them to do. If you want the business to succeed, it might take a few failures in terms of hiring the wrong people or giving the wrong training before you hit on the right formula. Since the TV show, Joyce sees a different attitude to risk and failure. She says, "If you don't at least fail once, then you never know what could have happened. If you risk nothing, you gain nothing." Learning what to do better next time is a vital part of being successful for whatever you have defined as your goals. We looked earlier in the book about setting your own ideals of success. But these often change along the journey. The path from the beginning to the successful end will never be one without failures, no matter how small or large. Looking at the safety net all the time means that you are not looking at the success that can happen.

If we set ourselves up to never fail, then we are never in the position to achieve. Push through the fears that you have in your mind to get to the place you want to be. Failing isn't a backward step on the path. It is a forward step that eliminates something from the playbook. This is stated perfectly by Joyce, "You fail forward. Because you are gonna learn a better way each time, learn a way not to do it for next time. Ultimately this takes you closer to your goal." This is a beautiful way of looking at the concept of failing to success. It encapsulates everything we are looking at in this book.

You never go into situations with failure as an option. We start out on a personal or business path looking at what we can do. But the mindset gets in the way. Joyce faced a series of uncomfortable challenges on the show. Nothing that was put in front of her was within her comfort zone. That's when we find out the most about ourselves. She said, "As long as I'm not dying or really hurting, then I'll push through. Each time I did, I was amazed at the outcome. I was so proud of myself. I had no idea I was capable of that. People put limitations on themselves, rather than pushing through their fear."

Giving yourself a challenge is one of the best gifts you can bestow upon yourself; rather than staying in that comfort zone that doesn't test your skills, your personality and your spirit, we should look outside of this. The saying is, "Anyone who has never made a mistake, has never tried anything new." I'm sure many of us are inspired by this quote. We might put it up on our social media timelines and feel a bit of inspiration when we read it, but that doesn't make a bit of difference unless we choose to live that life. Living within your comfort zone makes for an easy life, but possibly one that is unfulfilled. None of us want to look back on the life we lead and consider that we didn't fulfill our potential. I think that could possibly be the worst thing in the world. To move on to the next level, we must try things that we don't honestly know we are capable of. The move to the next level is one of learning and experimentation. Never be afraid to do this.

Joyce has moved on from The Amazing Race to a life of inspiring others. From these televised acts of failure, she is in a position now where many would consider her as a winner. She could have gone into her shell after the initial failures. She could have been one of those people who were defined by reality show television. We can all probably remember at least one of these. But she knew that each failure was a step towards the success she craved. She always kept the long-term goal in mind, so the small failures along the way were never going to define her. She wasn't overwhelmed by the loss, but knew that was going to help her work out what she wanted to be.

In fact, she doesn't define these as failures any longer. She sees them as helping her to succeed. Getting closer every day to your goals doesn't necessarily have to mean a big stride forward every day. It was Thomas Edison who said that he hadn't failed – just discovered another way that didn't work. We should walk into every situation with this attitude. Fearing the consequences of a single failure can cause us to freeze and not move forward. It can hinder us from trying something out to see if it works.

Joyce looks at it in this way, "I would have never known what I could have accomplished if I hadn't kept going. I kept going over every hurdle, crying, being scared even terrified, but this was the only way I was going to be able to accomplish my goal." That goal was accomplished in the TV show and in life. She is very proud of her achievements, and rightly should be.

We will leave the chapter with a quote from Joyce, winner of the 7th season of The Amazing Race, "Absolutely you have to fail in order to win." You can't say it better than that.

As we can see, TV can be a daunting place to fail and succeed. It isn't just The Amazing Race where this happens.

Lisa D'Amato has been a winner and a failure in a very public way on TV. She was crowned America's Next Top Model All Star Cycle, a triumph that changed her life overnight.

But with fame comes pressure. Lisa ended up back on television a few years later on a program called Celebrity Rehab. Airing these demons in public takes a whole lot of courage. It is about the right mindset, the one that allows us to accept failure as a lesson and move on.

Dealing with addiction takes character anyway. Doing this under the glare of the cameras adds another dimension. But Lisa bounced back to another TV success.

Shark Tank is another high-pressure TV show. One that Lisa might have been forgiven for avoiding. But she faced the potential grilling from potential investors to walk away with investment. She made the deal!

That's the way to approach the pressures of life – just keep coming back for more.

Lisa and Joyce, we salute you!

DREAM IT, NEVER FEAR IT & START LIVING IT!

When you have a vision and a dream, you need to check your ego at the door. That's what Lisa and Joyce did. Ego and pride are the enemies to success and innovation. Do you care about what others think of you? How does that get in the way of going for your dreams?

Is worry over what others think of you (if you fail) stopping you from going for your dreams? If your mission and vision are bigger than your concerns about what others might think of you, then you will be able to overcome your fears. Also, I have news for you, nobody's thinking of you.

What are the five things you can do right now that will take you out of your comfort zone? Make a list and then do them. How did it feel? How did you grow from the experience?

Are you truly willing to do whatever it takes to bring your idea to life? It's easy to start a company with an attitude that you are willing to do whatever it takes to make it successful. When you are put to the test, that's the moment that separates the winners from the losers and Lisa and Joyce are inspirations for no job being beneath them and for not caring about what others will think of them.

> "Every search begins with beginner's luck, and every search ends with the victor's being severely tested."
> — Paulo Coelho, The Alchemist

PART 9

THE MOST FAILING PLAYER IN THE HISTORY OF BASKETBALL

IF YOU LEARN FROM YOUR FAILURES, YOU'VE REALLY WON!

PATRICK WILLIAMS

PART 9 – MOST FAILING PLAYER IN BASKETBALL

Whether you have little knowledge about the game of basketball or are an avid fan with encyclopedic knowledge, I'd like you to have a think about the player who has failed the most times in the history of the game.

Take a few seconds to think and then come back to this page. You're probably thinking about some player who nearly made it to the NBA but was robbed by injury. Or a guy who was in and around the team for years but rarely made the starting 5, had little impact from the bench and never got to the playoffs. Or you might think about someone who had all the talent in the world and let their private life get out of control.

You're wrong on all counts. The player that has failed the most times in the NBA is none other than Michael Jordan. He missed more shots than he made. His career average success rate was 49.7% - this for a man who is almost unanimously seen as the greatest of all time. That's where the beauty lies. The players that you might have come up with when brainstorming the most failing player of all time didn't take a tiny fraction of the shots that MJ did. They were never put in the position of the ultimate microcosm of the game of basketball, or any sport – score and you win, miss and you lose. If you want to see success and failure, then watch the last few seconds of a close game of basketball, especially one that matters like a playoff game.

That's you in life. The times where it really matters is where you should step up and take control of the game. The top teams look for someone who is going to make the shot.

So, who's the guy they go to every time? It's the one that knows there is such a fine line between success and failure. The players on the team that look the other way when the coach is looking for someone to step up to the plate are more afraid of failure than they are inspired by success. Jordan knew that his career average was around 50%, so he knew that he had a

50-50 chance of making the shot. All the practice in the world doesn't take away all the factors at play:

- The pressure of the situation
- The impact of your opponent
- The bounce of the ball

And so, you have a choice to make. You can be like the rest of the team, looking up to the star player hoping to make the shot or you can 'be like Mike' and try to influence the game. They say that everybody wants to be like Mike, so prove it when there are tough decisions or situations. Be the player that everyone else looks up to.

Let's get the great man to give us a little more background to this:

> "I've missed more than 9,000 shots in my career. I've lost almost 300 games. Twenty-six times, I've been trusted to take the game winning shot and missed. I've failed over and over and over again in my life, and that is why I succeed."

And that's the attitude that saw him get tossed the ball from the side-lines every single time there was a pressure play. The opposition knew it was going to MJ. The rest of the team knew what was going to happen. So, it was down to Michael to decide what his destiny was going to be. If he had taken a back seat and looked for someone else on the team to make the play, then we wouldn't talk about him with such reverence even over a decade after he retired. He is the greatest, but many of his teammates have as many Championship rings as the great man. So, why don't we remember them with as much fondness? They were not in the same mold.

PART 9 – MOST FAILING PLAYER IN BASKETBALL 73

The quote above shows that being aware of the need to fail in order to succeed has given Jordan the ability to relax into his role. Building pressure because you are the go-to guy would have probably affected his performance negatively, and this can happen to you in your personal or business life too.

Understand that you might not make all the shots you take. But you will most definitely not score from all the ones you chose not to take. Not deciding because it is tough does nothing to make that choice any easier. On the very odd occasion, the problem will go away by itself with no outside intervention. But two things are happening here:

1. You are leaving things to chance

2. You haven't learned how to deal with that situation next time it arises

And failing is just this. We know what not to do next time. We get a feel for how we could have done things better. Asking others you trust to give input on how you perform is a great way to build this picture. After the event, when the dust has settled, gain feedback from others on what you did well and what you could have done better. This is how we learn.

Life is a series of events that we can often have little or no control over. So, we roll with the punches and adapt. The next time we face the same thing, there is a better understanding of the world and how to deal with it. MJ understood this, and just kept on doing what he was great at, but the stats show that he failed more than any other player in history. So, you can see that this is a mindset. Let the weight of the world sit on your shoulders and you can start down a path where you stop taking risks, stop being vibrant and stop moving forward. In the business world, this is a dangerous thing. Not moving forward means that you are being left behind.

We're not all Michael Jordan, that's for sure. We aren't all 6'6" tall, with hands the size of a bear! It's not only in basketball that we might come up short. Whatever dream you are chasing, I'm sure you could come up with all manner of reasons why you can't achieve it. But it's not those reasons that matter. It's what you do that matters.

Action trumps inaction every day of the week. Michael Jordan acted. He stepped up to the plate and shouldered the pressure of the rest of the team, the coach, the owners and the fans.

FAILURES AREN'T AN END, THEY'RE ONLY "STEPS" TOWARDS SUCCESS

How many shots did Michael Jordan have to take to get a basket? How many games did he have to lose to eventually win a championship?

Here's how you can apply these questions to your business. How many "no's" does it take to get to one "yes?"

How many failures does it take to get to that one success? It takes a lot! Every failure takes you one step closer to reaching your goals. Don't let failure stop you!!!

PART 10

THE CLICHÉ OF THE STRUGGLING ARTIST

STRUGGLING STRENGTHENS YOU! IT DOESN'T HOLD YOU BACK!

PATRICK WILLIAMS

PART 10 – THE CLICHÉ OF THE STRUGGLING ARTIST

If you think about some of the great masters of art over the centuries, then the kind of names that roll off the tongue include people such as Toulouse-Lautrec, Gauguin, Rembrandt van Rijn, Vermeer and Vincent Van Gogh.

Their paintings now sell for millions upon millions of dollars whenever they come up at auction. Their masterpieces are housed in the most notable of art galleries across the globe, drawing huge numbers of visitors to take in the sheer wonder and beauty of their art.

One thing that runs as a common thread with all these artists is that they struggled during their lifetime, and all died pretty much penniless. There is often a connection made between art and struggle, and this is where we can see the long-lasting effect of a real legacy.

It would have been easy for all these artists to pack up their easels and go away to do something else that took up less time and paid better than art, but they were not in it for the dollars! These artists were carrying out what they viewed as their life's work. Even though others at the time could not see the value or importance of the paintings these artists and others delivered to the world, centuries later, we are marvelling at what they were able to produce.

It is important to understand that your legacy may not be readily evident to others after the first few days, weeks, months or even years of your struggle. Paintings that were seen as failures, both in terms of the art and the commerciality, are now exchanged for tens or even hundreds of millions of dollars. What you build today might not have an intrinsic value based on what value you have built, but the potential for the future is what you should keep your eye on.

The fact that these works of art had very little interest at the time would have been enough to deter the vast majority of people.

This book is aimed at people who think differently about their life's work. Trying to appeal to others feels like an essential element of what we do with our business or personal goals. Pleasing others in your personal life is a natural way to gain satisfaction. Pleasing others in the commercial world means that your product or service is on the road to success.

But, in the early days at least, you need to look elsewhere for the goals that will define the way you develop over time. You must look at the legacy that you will leave behind. This is the same way that these artists developed their work.

If the long-term aim is to make a product that everyone loves, then you are already on to becoming a loser. Not everybody likes any one thing. There are always dissenters, and in business that's just fine. Unless your profit margins are so slim that you need seven billion people to buy from you, then you don't have to appeal to everyone. By the way, if your profit margins are that slim, then up your prices!

You want to appeal to the right group. It has taken far longer than their lifetime, but the artists listed above, such as Van Gogh and Vermeer were appealing to those that really understood art. It feels from this far away that they always knew the importance of their work. To be able to look at these paintings hundreds of years after their death and marvel at the quality of what they did is truly amazing. They have delivered something that will resonate throughout the ages. They have created something far more important than commercial success in their own lifetime. They were not put off by the failures they had during their lifetime. They were able to keep to the vision and produce something extraordinary.

But, of course, we live in different times. If we can create something truly amazing today, then there is a ready audience out there waiting to take it in, and we shouldn't be afraid to

PART 10 – THE CLICHÉ OF THE STRUGGLING ARTIST

fail on the way. So, rather than trying to appeal to the lowest common denominator, we should try to appeal to the best in people. We should be prepared to aim as high as we can, and to fail on the way, when necessary.

Failure is a vital part of success. These artists could have painted a few portraits, seen little in return and then just walked away from the craft forever. The world would be a much poorer place because of it. We maybe wouldn't have access to some of the most revered paintings in the world today. We never know when that break might come. We never know the legacy we are leaving behind. There are probably hundreds of successful businesses out there that didn't get off the ground because the owners ran out of patience or backed out after a failure or two. Just sticking with it could have converted them into millionaires or beyond. But, if you don't keep the long-term squarely in view all the time, then you can easily become distracted by a setback here and there. It feels overwhelming and it is far easier to just go away and do something less risky instead.

Mindset plays such a heavy role in our life. You might hear the phrase "she always lands on her feet" and think that luck is the most important factor in success. But if you never freefall, then you won't ever be in a position where landing on your feet is an option. In short, you have to let the ground disappear from under you every now and again. It's the only way you will learn how to land at all.

If you land on your ass the first few times, nobody cares. It's all part of the learning curve. Landing on your ass helps you to think about how you can land on your feet the next time, while always keeping the end goal in view.

These artists developed over time. Look at their early work and you will see a lot of art that doesn't really amount to much. The colors aren't well matched, the lines are kind of fuzzy and the style is all over the place. But they were just at the start of their journey. They didn't paint a masterpiece the first occasion they picked up a brush.

They learned all about their craft before developing their own style. Most of us can pick a Rembrandt or a Van Gogh if we see it, certainly from their later work. This style developed as they practiced, found new ways of doing things and became the supreme artists.

You need to be able to do this for yourself.

And this is a vitally important lesson when it comes to failing to success. You have to be easy on yourself. Not to the point where you don't care about the results, but never beat yourself up for failing. It is a vital part of the process, and one that leads to success.

Make a mistake and that's fine, if you learn from it. Keep making the same mistake and you are not making any progress at all. Every mistake should turn into a different output. If you make subtle changes then you can end up with a wildly successful thing at the end of it. That's what we are all trying to do.

Being tough on yourself because you have hit a little bump in the road just ramps up the pressure. This isn't something that leads to successful results. When we pile pressure on ourselves, the result is that we are afraid to take risks. If Van Gogh had never taken a risk, we wouldn't have The Sunflowers, and we would be in a world that was poorer for that.

It can be difficult to have the mindset of being easy on your failures. But the true path to success comes from those little setbacks that steer us in the right direction. Never think that you can't make a decision and hope that it is right. All the research in the world sometimes doesn't give you a waterproof solution that you are 100% sure will work. That's life. Try something, see if it works and make changes if it doesn't.

We are constantly refining what we do. Much of this comes from the subconscious level of the brain. It is programmed to make all of those fine adjustments that keep us balanced, process information and link the brain with the movements of the body. Think about your route to success in very much the same way.

Getting better at what you do is something that we all aspire to. But, without setting those goals and not being afraid to fail, you never make sufficient progress. Very often, subtle changes can bring about big successes.

Life is a series of lessons, and the sooner we pick this up, the easier it gets. Making a few mistakes usually doesn't harm you. In business, making them when you are small is a fantastic way to build up knowledge that will help you in the future.

Imagine how much money Coca-Cola would have saved if they tried the new formula when they were a small company. It doesn't bear thinking about.

So, be like an artist. Think about the people you can inspire and the brilliance you can bring to the world. To achieve this, you must take a few risks. Paint large across your own version of the world what you want to achieve. Tell as many other people as will listen, as you build your legacy. Others will feed off your passion and join you. Being an artist means you get to try so many new things in route to your final destination.

FIND YOUR NICHE PASSION & PRESS THE ACCELERATOR TO THE FLOOR

What makes these artists stand out is that they found their authentic voice and expressed it unapologetically. They had their critics and it didn't deter them. They chose the road less travelled.

Gauguin went to Tahiti and painted the native people and their culture through the lens of a French Impressionist. He left his wife and his life behind to pursue his calling and live an exotic life surrounded by customs that were foreign to him. From this unique vision came a blend of French Impressionism with primitive Tahitian expressiveness and colors. His art is lively and different from all his French counterparts.

What are you doing differently from everyone else out there? What experiences allow you to see things differently?

PART 11

MEASURING SUCCESS – WHERE DOES IT START?

FROM THE START, MEASURE EVERY STEP TO TRACK YOUR GAINS

PATRICK WILLIAMS

PART 11 – MEASURING SUCCESS / WHERE DOES IT START?

It can be really difficult to define success. Some see it as reaching a goal that was aimed for at some time in the past, but this doesn't consider that all manner of things that can happen along the way.

More importantly, it only works if you have a clearly defined goal and a measured starting point. We don't always have that. The borders are fuzzy.

They say that we are the sum of all our experiences. If that is the case, then how can we define the starting point for our journey? For many successful people, they point to a time in their childhood or schooling that started them on the path to success.

But for many more, the way we are taught in school is marked with failure.

Dan Smith: Author of *FAILING GREATLY: Your Guide to Achieving Success after Failure* looks intently at the school system in the United States as one of the reasons we are not set up to embrace failure as part of the learning process:

"Dan had great insight and very different way to look at failure and success.

His thoughts about failure starts in the schools with kids receiving letter grades A-F.

Why do we use the letter "A" for a grade that means you have succeeded or done well when the letter "A" doesn't stand for anything?

The letter grade system is A-F, and you skip the letter "E" and the letter "E" stands for excellence. The letter "F" stands for failing or failure and we begin learning the word failure at an early age. I think that the word failure should be replaced with the letter "L" for learning. I also think that we should reward effort more than the actual part of achievement because if you don't learn lessons along the way as part of the process than we are not really achieving the goal of success because we had no mistakes or failure in the process."

Schools are measured on their performance, so they feel it is right to pass this down the line and measure their pupils on their performance. There is no easier measure than academic results. It is an easy way to set a standard and then measure how closely the school gets to that standard.

In every way, that doesn't include the vital information about the starting point for every single student in that school. Those that have learning difficulties, problems at home or don't feel inspired by the present system become a problem rather than an opportunity. Teachers are incentivized to get all their students to a certain level, so see the process as exactly that – a process. What is all that about?

Success and failure are etched on the brains of our kids from an early age. We don't want them to fail in the long run, but if we don't let them have those little failures in the early years then they don't develop the capacity to analyze the failure, think it through and provide a solution that will prevent it next time. This means we are raising a generation of children that don't know what it is like to experience failure until they leave school and walk out into the big bad world. That's not right.

As Dan Smith says, the marking of schoolwork in the present system shows an 'F' should be avoided at all costs. It is the lowest of the low and ridiculed by the rest of the class. But what if the "failure" of one person in the class could provide a learning point for the rest of them? What if we embraced the learning and moved forward as a group of people? Now that would change the way we looked at the world.

PART 11 – MEASURING SUCCESS / WHERE DOES IT START?

We all accept that the start of our life journey is hugely influential on the rest of it. The way we are brought up to understand and decipher the world in the first few years of life and the first few years of schooling shape the way we interact with the world for all our days. The exceptions are where people experience major life altering events that can override the conditioning we experience in our younger days.

So why do we accept the fact that failure has become a dirty word in our schools? Why do we want our kids to pass every lesson with flying colors? The answer isn't as simple as might first appear.

There are so many ways in which we can support our kids. Society has us conditioned (in many ways from the distant past) that we need to compete with others in order to get ahead. As much as there is a movement out there about helping others, there is always that underlying feeling that we need to win to stay ahead. With winners, there are inevitably losers, and nobody wants that title.

So, we push our kids to get the best scores, perform at the top of their game in sports or to be often what we wanted to be when we were younger but never quite made it. If you wanted to be a basketball star in your school days but didn't quite make the grade, then you will push your kids harder in search of that dream. It is kind of natural that you would think that way.

Kids that lose a full season of little league games feel like they are useless. Unless they have a great coach, one who explains to them the benefits of losing week after week. The season might end with a 0-17 loss record or end with a 3-2 ninth inning defeat. The progress in between can be marked and shown as the road to success in the following campaign. Guess what happens? They not only break that losing streak, but also know how it feels when they come across another team on the same path the following season. These kids not only become better players but can empathize with their peers. Quite an impressive life lesson from a few games of little league baseball.

We don't do this often enough. Shouting at our big league team from the sideline every week feels like winning is the be all and end all. Jimi Wilson said, "I don't want to be remembered as an average ball player, I want to be remembered as the best to ever step on a diamond." If we carry this attitude in isolation to everything our kids do, then we are heading for a fall. It creates cheaters, it creates bad losers and, most importantly, it creates kids who are not ready for all the challenges that life throws their way. That's not a fair way to bring children into the world.

Embrace the failure of your kids. Understand that they are not perfect, they are not winning machines. If they make a mistake, then help them to understand that it is OK to make a mistake. It is OK to slip up every now and again on their path to wherever they want to be.

So, that begs the question - Where does it start? Where do you begin to measure your road to success?

The path that we are looking at in this book embraces the failures along the way. The beginning of the road is when you make a decision (decide to decide as they say in business circles) on what you want to achieve. Then you define that goal in some detail and work through the gears to get there. That is your starting point.

As Marcus Aurelius put it nearly 2000 years ago, "The impediment to action advances action. What stands in the way becomes the way."

MAKE IT FUN ... THAT'S A MUST!

It's all about the journey, and not the destination. Embrace the journey and all the failures that are part and parcel to achieving your goals. If you don't enjoy the process, then why bother. When you do something that you love, it never feels like you've worked a day in your life.

Surround yourself with people who inspire you and that you enjoy working with. Nothing can be more rewarding than enjoying the work that you do and being surrounded by people who are competent and great to work with.

Keep in mind the story about the fisherman versus the man who works 360 days a year so that he can take a fishing vacation.

PART 12

THE REMARKABLE STORY OF THOMAS A. EDISON

FAILURE TEACHES US MORE THAN ALL OF OUR SUCCESSES

PATRICK WILLIAMS

PART 12 – REMARKABLE STORY OF THOMAS A. EDISON

Probably, the godfather of failing to success is Thomas Alva Edison. We all know him as a successful inventor who brought many different ideas to life. They say that Edison could imagine a machine in his mind and operate it years before he was able to bring that idea to life. He has brought us the technology of the electric lightbulb and the phonograph, as well as holding over 1,000 patents for various designs that he came up with over time.

I'm sure you are reading this book thinking, "How can you write a book about failing to success and include someone who has probably never failed in his life?"

But Edison was a serial failure. In fact, he embraced failure as an essential part of his success.

> "Our greatest weakness lies in giving up.
> The most certain way to succeed is always
> to try just one more time."

And that is the most remarkable thing about us as human beings. We are often scared to take one more try because failure hurts. Going again and again at something that doesn't work is a painful process. We know that others will be looking at what we do, ready to let us know we haven't got it right. But as long as we are learning from every failure and refine what we do, then success is an inevitable outcome, given a long enough timeline. That's what we do as individuals: we keep on going when it looks like there is no point. We can do it when we are faced with absolute adversity, but we need to make this mindset a habit – do it every day. I know you can.

You have heard of the product WD-40, right? You may have wondered from time to time how it wound up with that particular name. Well, WD-40 was the 40th attempt by the manufacturer to get the product just right and ready for market. The first formulation was called WD-1, and that was the one they intended to take to the market and make a boatload of cash. The fact that the owners of the product were willing and able to keep on going, refining the product as they went, gave them the best-selling product they have today. Giving up at formulation 39 because they had failed too many times would have put them so near and yet so far from success.

We tend to think of success as an overnight thing. We think that an artist, athlete or business owner has risen to success from absolutely nothing. Of course, this is far from the case. Behind every champion track and field athlete that wins an Olympic Gold for their country, there are hours spent training, busting a gut to become the best they can be.

> **"There may be people who have more talent than you, but there's no excuse for anyone to work harder than you do ... and I believe that."**
> — Derek Jeter

There is nothing overnight about an overnight success.

And the same goes with Thomas Alva Edison. The way we can look back at history with the benefit of massive hindsight means that we can look at his overall body of work. Dropping into Edison's life in the early years of his inventing might have led you to believe that this man would never amount to anything. Seeing a pile of discarded ideas and failed inventions could have made you think that this was someone wasting their life away inventing useless things just for the sake of it.

But that would be to underestimate the mindset of the man. His continual path toward excellence was underpinned by his positive mental attitude. He didn't get put off by failure but was

PART 12 – REMARKABLE STORY OF THOMAS A. EDISON

inspired by it. We can choose the way that events shape us in a way that we cannot choose the events.

Failing at something once or twice isn't a problem for many people. They might see some big areas for improvement after the first go and then develop ways to counter these issues. But failing more than a handful of times will put most people off trying ever again. Imagine failing hundreds or even thousands of times. This sends shivers up and down the spine for all but a tiny few. But, if the path of these thousands of failures is linked to progress, there is no reason to be downhearted.

Think back briefly to the movie *Groundhog Day* starring Bill Murray. He is stuck in a continuous loop of the same day, witnessing the same events and making new decisions on what best to do to win a love interest over. Your life is the same. But, unlike the character Phil Connors in the movie, you don't get an endless series of days to get it right. You need to treat every day like it is the most precious gift – it is! Work out how to make everything all right and get the girl (or guy) by trying time and time again to succeed. If Bill Murray's character gave up and stayed in bed, then it wouldn't be much of a movie – and he wouldn't have much of a life.

> "Just because something doesn't do what you planned it to do doesn't mean it's useless."
> — Thomas A. Edison

We often get stuck in the mindset that it is success or nothing. We hear that all the time. Second place is first loser. No, it isn't. Second place is a stepping stone for many, but an achievement for many too. Clouding our minds with the loser or failure mentality creates a world where we become afraid to take any risk at all because it might lead down the wrong path. There is no wrong path if you look at the difference between success and failure through the right lens.

Thomas Edison didn't live to see the eventual fruition of his work. Nor did any of the artists we looked at earlier in the book. But they knew the higher purpose of what they were doing. The legacy we leave behind is a far greater motivating factor than an immediate hint of that 'sweet smell of success'. It doesn't evaporate anywhere near as quickly as the short burst of a simple win. It doesn't prepare you for the failures you might face as life goes on. You should look at the long-term view rather than the easy hits. But we are aware that your long-term view will be two things:

1. Something that can and should be broken down into smaller achievable goals along the way
2. There will be several failures on the way

That is what this book is all about. We are not afraid of making a few mistakes on the road to the big vision we have. You could say from reading about his life that Edison was obsessed with hard work. There are many quotes related to this if you conduct a short search of the internet:

"Opportunity is missed by most people because it is dressed in overalls and looks like work."

This theme runs alongside his attitude to failure. If you work hard at something, that is if it doesn't come naturally easy to you, then you will make at least a few mistakes. You will get things wrong and that is OK. In fact, that is more than OK in the eyes of Edison. It is a necessary part of the process of getting to where you want to be.

That is the mindset we should all embrace. Stop thinking that you must succeed at every small task you try. Some of them won't matter. But most of them will – in the most positive way. Edison would never have invented the electric lightbulb without first understanding how to NOT make it. The knowledge wasn't already out there, at least in any way he could have accessed. So, he did the next best thing. He tested and experimented until he built the knowledge himself. This happened day by day, piece by piece, failure by failure.

PERSEVERE, YOU CAN DO IT!

Every time you have a failure or setback, make a list of 5-10 more steps you can take to move you towards your goal.

What new idea can you experiment with? How can you do it differently this time?

Now that you know what NOT to do, what can you do next? "Where there is a will, there is a way."

PART 13

THE SHORTCUT TO SUCCESS

SHORTCUTS CAN ALSO DELAY YOUR SUCCESS! SO, DON'T TAKE 'EM!

PATRICK WILLIAMS

PART 13 – THE SHORTCUT TO SUCCESS

We hear it all the time. There are 'get rich quick' schemes all over the Internet. We all want to be able to make money without the effort. We are all looking for the shortcut to success. I can tell you now, it doesn't exist. If you want to get rich without putting any real effort in, then buy a lottery ticket. But you must accept that the chances of winning are one in tens of millions or even more, and the fact is that you stand more chance of being struck by lightning.

The idea of a shortcut to success is a symptom of a society where we see success and failure at every turn.

The news tells stories of failure. Bad news sells.

Celebrity magazines tell stories of success. Glamour sells.

We don't see any of the journey from one place to the other. Those people whose lifestyles we envy splashed across TV or one of the celebrity magazines don't tell a story. They are a snapshot in time, of a person knowing they are being watched. They show off all they have in that moment. There is nothing of the struggle to get where they are, or even the struggle they are facing at that particular point in time. We want some of the success, and we don't see the struggle.

So, we all look for a shortcut. We want that lifestyle we see – and don't want to put any work into it happening. Many of the people we see live this glamorous lifestyle are in the entertainment industry or sports stars. It appears easy to sing a song or act in a movie and make it big. How easy is it? Well, ask all the struggling actors waiting tables or appearing as extras in Los Angeles. The place is literally filled with them. That is a sure indication that it isn't easy at all.

There is no shortcut.

That's as simple as I can put it. There is no way that is guaranteed success without making any mistakes at all. You need to be able to accept failure for what it is and roll with it. The stories of the successful should act as inspiration for you, but not cloud the fact that you must work hard and make a bunch of mistakes to get to where you want to be in life.

Mistakes are a good thing; tell yourself that. They help you to understand what won't work. They help you to narrow the field of possibilities until you have the one that works. When you get that mindset sorted, then you start to understand what all of this is about. There is something out there for all of us, I truly believe that. There is something that you can do as well as the best in the world and make boatloads of money from. It is out there. But unless you start trying the possibilities then you have no idea what that thing is.

Imagine if Michael Jordan decided he couldn't play basketball and didn't even try.

Think about a world where Martin Luther King decided he couldn't make a change – and didn't even try.

Imagine if Steve Jobs went to work for someone else.

Consider a world where Dr. Seuss didn't keep talking about his books to others.

All of these scenarios could have easily happened. We were only a small change away from one of these things happening. The way that our world works is that there are a million alternatives for what actually happens. It is your duty to explore these alternatives for your life and your career. Don't stop at trying once or twice, try a thousand times. If that doesn't give you the result, then try a million times. Always make sure that you give it your all but try and work through the possibilities. It is about having

PART 13 – THE SHORTCUT TO SUCCESS

the attitude where you don't say, "no" to any opportunity. We have become predisposed to shy away from risk, from anything we haven't tried before.

We want to go with a friend, read the reviews online or find someone who has done it before. From there we can be easily talked out of it. We can decide that the risk isn't worth it. Unless we are talking about sitting in a den of snakes, then the risk is probably going to be worth it. Even if that is just to cross something off the list that doesn't work for us.

I would say that you need to consider trying something new every week. It will change the way you view the world from one of a series of potential risks to a series of potential opportunities, and if you fail while you are trying something new then so be it. It's something new – so what if you get it wrong? Nobody is here to judge you. Don't judge yourself.

There is no elevator to success – you have to take the stairs. It might sound like a cliché, but it is true. If you are not fit enough to climb all the stairs at once, then you need to take a few at a time. You might slip on the way. You might get to a point where there is no handrail. You might not be able to see around the next corner. You might have to carry something heavy, or someone heavy. Whatever it is that is causing you a problem on the way up those stairs is another opportunity to learn. It is your chance to find out how to climb those stairs with these impediments in the future. Once you know how to climb without the handrail once, then this isn't an issue the next time it comes up.

Champion athletes don't make things easier when they train. If you are going to be a marathon runner, then you don't train by running a few hundred yards and feeling that you can do the rest on the big day. Most marathon runners at the top-level train by running for 80 miles per week or more. Some train for more than 100 miles every single week, until they get close to the big day. This prepares them for all the rigors of a marathon. They know what is coming because they have trained over and over. Once they are in competition, they have the confidence to tackle these things.

Therefore, failure is so important. If you have never failed before an important event, then you don't know what to do if a problem arises. You don't know how to cope with all life throws at you.

Think about the person you admire most in the world. Imagine them in their prime, at the peak of their powers. It feels like they are invincible, doesn't it? They are not. They have reached this level of competence by making a complete mess of things in the past. They know what they are doing because they spent so much time not knowing a thing.

And that is where the inquisitive mind comes in. Being the person who freely admits they know nothing is a refreshing attitude to have. You may have met people like this in the past and think that they come across as a fools. They are clearly not.

When you start from a base of zero knowledge (or at least tell yourself this) then you can approach each new event with the mindset that exploration and failure are a natural part of what you do next.

Researching and then trying out the different methods or solutions is the best way to find an answer that fits you best. Without that level of experimentation, all you do is look on Google for the answers that other people have come up with. These might not work for you.

PART 14

HURRY UP AND FAIL!

FAILING FAST CAN ALSO BRING ABOUT LEARNING, NOT JUST SUCCESS

PATRICK WILLIAMS

PART 14 – HURRY UP AND FAIL!

None of this can come quickly enough. What exactly are you waiting for? The longer we procrastinate and beat around the bush, the longer it is going to be until we find the right answers. If you want success, then you should not only be prepared for failure – you should get out there and fail as quickly as you possibly can!

> **"I failed in some subjects in the exam, but my friend passed in all. Now he is an engineer in Microsoft and I am the owner of Microsoft."** — Bill Gates

You need to know what works for you, and you need to know this information as soon as humanly possible. Hanging around just leaves a void that is filled by the status quo. Nothing great comes from the status quo. Even the most successful people (see Bill Gates above) start to edge closer to failure when they stop taking risks and pushing boundaries. The most successful people are always trying new things, putting themselves out of their comfort zone and looking for the next adventure. It is a natural part of this to mess up every now and again. You really shouldn't care about these failures. Look at them for inspiration in the future. Look at them for the path to success. Look at them for the lessons they are.

Look back on your life of adventure where you embrace those things we call mistakes. They are the things that define us as who we are. Without showing off our mistakes we are pretty much the same as the person next to us. Nobody wants to be the same as everyone else in the world. You are unique. Your mistakes confirm this. Hide them and you risk hiding the very fabric of your being. There are no reasons to hide anything you have done from the world. You are the person you have become because of all of the interaction and experience you have mustered over the years. You are not doing yourself credit by shying away from them.

So, what are you waiting for? There is a course run at Stanford University entitled FAIL FAST, FAIL OFTEN, and it is this kind of refreshing attitude to life that will see us move forward in every aspect. Get out there and fail today. Then do it again tomorrow, and the next day, the one after that, next week, month and year. Fail as often as you can for the rest of your life.

YOUR JOB IS TO FAIL, LOVE IT, GROW FROM IT AND EMBRACE IT BECAUSE IT ULTIMATELY LEADS TO SUCCESS

Really, nothing more needs to be said. That title above said it all. Well, we could just repeat the title of this chapter ...

"HURRY UP ... AND FAIL!"

SUMMARY WRAP-UP!

Book Patrick Williams
To Speak To Your Group About Failing To Succeed!

If the topic of FAILING TO SUCCESS inspires you, allow Patrick to inspire your team, group, company or audience!

Patrick speaks to groups of 15 to 15,000 on the principles of FAILING TO SUCCESS.

To book Patrick to speak, contact him through his website:

Failing2Success.com

FAILURE WRAP-UP & WORDS OF ENCOURAGEMENT

Now you know that failure is just as much a part of success as hard work, determination, planning, execution and the journey that it takes you to reach any goal.

How do you feel about failure now after reading so much on it? It is my hope that you begin to embrace failure as a natural part of the journey towards your success.

While there can and will be failures toward any of your pursuits, it's that single goal of success towards a goal that we're all after.

So, take action, go for it, stay the course, don't give up and no matter what failures might come your way... YOU WILL SUCCEED!

In advance, here's to all your failures and your future SUCCESS!

Genuinely,

Patrick Williams

PATRICK WILLIAMS
FOUNDER / SPEAKER
Failing2Success.com

www.ingramcontent.com/pod-product-compliance
Lightning Source LLC
Chambersburg PA
CBHW071416210526
45465CB00001B/410